Grilling

Cool Food for Hot Days

> Author: **Annette Heisch** | Photos: **Brigitte Sauer**

Contents

The Essentials

The Recipes

Appendix

Summertime is Grilling Time

Everybody loves the sound of sizzling on the grill because there's almost no preparation needed, everyone can help and you can look forward to enjoying a delicious meal with friends and family. Enjoy the simplicity of outdoor cooking using these new recipe ideas that include classic meat, elegant fish and sophisticated vegetable dishes. Tangy marinades and quick sauces help spice up the humdrum of everyday life and food. It's so easy to create a Mediterranean atmosphere right in your own backyard. Come barbecue with us!

Grilling Equipment and Accessories

Hibachi or Small Grill

Charcoal briquettes smolder in this small rectangular or round grill as the food sizzles on the rack above. You can choose from a wide variety of grills ranging from simple, inexpensive models to deluxe high-grade steel varieties. Portable, fold-up mini-grills are also available for barbecuing while on the road.

Advantages: Extremely light and portable, can be used anywhere.

Disadvantage: It takes a long time to get the coals ready.

Tip: Choose a grill that allows you to adjust the height of the rack, has insulated, non-metal handles and is easy to clean. Be sure to dispose of the ashes properly.

Covered Kettle

Another type of charcoal-fired grill but typically round and larger than a hibachi. They also permit barbecuing by indirect heat; in this case, the charcoal is heaped on two sides instead of directly under the food and the lid reflects the heat rising from below back onto the food. This method is most suited for large cuts of meat.

Advantages: Economical use of charcoal, cover also permits barbecuing in bad weather.

Important: Make sure the air vents are open when you start the fire.

Gas-Fired Grill

The fuel is supplied by a propane tank or bottle connected to the barbecue. There are two common types of gas grill: One has lava rocks under the rack that are heated by the gas burner. In the other, the gas flames are located under angled bars made of enameled steel. Both types are lit by a built-in igniter.

Advantages: Ready to use after heating only 10 minutes. Adjustable temperature. No odors caused by lighting. Easy to clean.

Disadvantages: More expensive and provide less of the aromatic, barbecue flavor. The igniters are occasionally know to fail after a few years of use.

Important: Always be sure to keep an extra propane tank on hand or know where the nearest filling station is. Occasionally you'll need to boil the lava rocks in water.

Electric Grill

To fire up this grill, just plug it in. The rack is heated by the coils below. A water pan is located beneath the coils to prevent over-heating.

Advantages: Easy to use and heats up quickly. No unpleasant smoke. Can also be used indoors and can be converted into a table-top grill.

Disadvantage: Can be used only where there an electrical outlet. Does not have the barbecue mystique.

Important: Choose a grill in which the heating coils are shielded the food won't drip onto them. And don't forget to add the water!

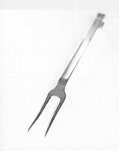   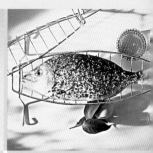

Barbecue Set

Tongs, a spatula and a fork, all with extra-long handles, let you turn meat, etc., without burning your fingers. **Important:** Make sure they are all metal with insulated handles.

Skewers

Wooden skewers are especially economical but have to be thrown away after each use, while metal skewers can be used again and again. **Important:** Soak wooden skewers in water for 15 minutes; grease metal skewers.

Basting Brush

You need a brush for basting meat, fish and vegetables with marinade. It's best to keep the brush handy in a cup or small bowl next to the grill along with the marinade. **Important:** Keep bristles away from direct heat and off of cooking rack so they do not melt

Fish Basket

If you frequently barbecue whole fish, you should buy a special fish basket. It makes turning the fish as easy as turning a hot dog. **Important:** Measure your grill to make sure the basket fits correctly.

Oven Mitts

Caution, hot and greasy! You need to protect your hands, especially when stirring the coals or turning hot metal skewers. **Important:** Buy mitts made of fire-retardant material.

Rotisserie

Whole chickens and rolled roasts are best roasted on a spit. The spit has to rotate continuously to distribute the heat evenly. A small battery-operated motor keeps it turning correctly.

Grill Brush

Special brushes with hard bristles make it easier to clean the rack. **Important:** Wear an oven mitt when grasping the hot rack or wait until it cools down. Always wait a few minutes after brushing to put food on rack.

Charcoal Starters

These come in a liquid, paste or solid form. Add starter to cold coals and never to coals that are burning. Make sure the starter has burned away completely before placing food on the rack.

Healthy Grilling

A sizzling grill and flickering flames may contribute to a romantic atmosphere but they do little to enhance the taste of your meat, fish or vegetables. Try to avoid creating smoke. Smoke forms when fat drips onto the coals and can produce hazardous substances .

1 | Cooking in Aluminum Grill Pans

These are ideal both for food that drips and for heat-sensitive items. The dripping fat or marinade collects in the grooves of the pan and doesn't drip onto the coals.
Additional benefit: The rack stays clean.
Important: Grease the pan with a high-heat cooking oil (e.g. corn or sunflower oil) so the food won't stick. Because the pan dampens the heat, grilling times will be a little longer.

Tip: For a more intense barbecue flavor, first cook the food in the grill pan and then, when it has cooked out most of its liquid, cook it briefly on the grill rack.

2 | Cooking in foil packets

This is a gentle method that is useful for vegetables, tender fish or meat wrapped in bacon, cabbage, etc.
Important: Wrap the food tightly so there's no dripping. Use either heavy-duty aluminum foil or a double layer of regular foil. Make sure the shiny side is on the inside so the heat will be reflected inward.

> 2 *You can wrap foods in aluminum foil ahead of time.*

3 | Vertical grilling

This requires a special grill in which the coals are layered vertically in a container. The heat radiates sideways onto the food that is also positioned vertically, either clamped into a basket or rotating on a spit, thus preventing any fat from dripping on the coals.

TIP
No matter what method you use, grilling is unsuitable for anything that's cured. You can recognize cured foods by their reddish color. Smoked pork, bacon and certain types of hot dogs and sausages have no business on a rack. High heat can release carcinogenic nitrite nitrosamine from the curing brine.

Fuel

Be sure to choose the right fuel when you grill. Charcoal briquettes are available from any supermarket, gas station or home improvement center during the summer season. Briquettes provide embers that last an especially long time and are always recommended for food with longer cooking times. If you only want to grill a few quick steaks or sausages, you can also use lump charcoal, which is not quite as readily available but can be found at hardware stores and larger home improvement centers. The fuel available in stores generally leaves no harmful residue. However, this may not be the case when burning wood or paper and it is therefore not recommended. If you want a classier type of fuel, beech and grape wood also make a good fire but take at least an hour to heat up.

1 Lighting the grill

Stack the fuel in a pyramid. Charcoal lighters such as liquid starters and small lighter cubes make it easier to ignite the fire. Use long matches available for grills and fire-places to ignite the coals.

2 Good coals

For these you need air, patience and at least half an hour. The best method is to let the coals burn slowly until they are covered with a layer of white ash.

3 Grill rack

Brush the rack with a high-heat cooking oil so the food won't stick. The coals should be 4 inches from the rack. For longer cooking times, increase the distance and then move the rack closer to the fire in the final stages.

4 Correct cooking time

Specified cooking times are approximations and fluctuate depending on the heat of your grill and size of the food. Fish, poultry and pork must be cooked thoroughly. Test them for doneness before serving.

Marinades and Seasonings

The Basic Ingredients

—Neutral, high-heat cooking oil such as corn, sunflower or peanut oil and mild olive oil
—Herbs, fresh or dried: Thyme, rosemary, oregano
—Spices: Black pepper, cayenne pepper, paprika (Hungarian sweet and hot), chili powder
—Seasoning sauces: Ketchup, chili sauce, Tabasco, Worcestershire
—Mustard, honey, lemons, tomato paste, garlic

Barbecue Sauce

For 4 servings:
2/3 cup ketchup
1 tbs red wine vinegar
3 tsp Worcestershire sauce
1 tsp honey
1 tsp medium-hot mustard
1 tsp Hungarian sweet paprika
1 tsp chili powder
Salt and pepper
Stir all these ingredients together thoroughly to form a sauce

Goes with: Beef, pork and poultry. This sauce can be used as a marinade and cooking sauce as well as a dip.

Spice Mixtures

Each recipe is for 8 servings:
Caribbean: $1/2$ tsp ground allspice, 1 tbs thyme, $1/4$ tsp grated nutmeg , $1/4$ tsp cinnamon

Indian: $1/2$ tsp ground cumin, $1/4$ tsp ground coriander, 4 pinches ground cloves, $1/4$ tsp cinnamon, $1/2$ tsp curry powder

Mediterranean: 1 tsp thyme, 1 tsp oregano, $1/2$ tsp rosemary

Hot Ginger Marinade

For 4 servings:
1 piece fresh ginger (about walnut-sized)
1 red chili pepper
4 crushed allspice berries (or $1/2$ tsp ground allspice)
2 tbs lime or lemon juice
6 tbs peanut oil

Peel ginger and chop finely. Clean chili pepper, rinse, pat dry and cut into rings. Stir together all ingredients

Goes with: Poultry, pork, fish

Red Wine Marinade

For 4 servings:
Squeeze 1 clove garlic through a press and stir together with ½ cup red wine, 4 tbs olive oil and 1 tbs tomato paste. Season to taste with black pepper.
Goes with: Beef and lamb

Thyme Oil

For 4 servings:
Stir together 1 tsp dried thyme, 1 tsp lemon juice, 5 tbs olive oil and ½ tsp pink peppercorns (optional).
Goes with: Lamb, poultry

Lemon Marinade

For 4 servings:
Stir together 2 tbs lemon juice, 1 pinch grated lemon zest, 1 tbs orange juice, 3 tbs corn oil and ½ tsp coarsely crushed fennel seeds (optional).
Goes with: Fish

Sherry Marinade

For 4 servings:
Stir together 1 tbs dry sherry, 2 tsp balsamic vinegar, 3 tbs olive oil and ½ tsp dried oregano.
Goes with: Poultry, pork

Rum Marinade

For 4 servings:
Squeeze 1 clove garlic through a press and stir together with 5 tbs olive oil, 2 tbs dark rum, ½ tsp chili powder, ¼ tsp crushed black pepper and 2 pinches cinnamon.
Goes with: Steaks

Asian Marinade

For 4 servings:
Stir together 3 tbs soy sauce, 3 tbs chicken stock, 1 tbs dark sesame oil, ½ tsp freshly grated ginger, 1 clove garlic squeezed through a press, 1 tsp lemon juice and 1 tsp honey.
Goes with: Pork

Sauces, Dips, Etc.

Prepared Sauces

It's helpful to keep these sauces on hand for last-minute barbecues and for whenever you don't have a lot of time. You'll find them at supermarkets and delis: Ketchup (traditional and a spicy variety), cocktail sauce, garlic puree, chili sauce and a variety of spicy relish. Asian and Middle-Eastern markets also offer satay sauce and various chutneys that can add personality to a wide variety of grilled items.

Tip: Spice up prepared sauces with a few fresh herbs.

Peanut Sauce

4 oz roasted, salted peanuts
1 1/2 oz solid coconut cream
2 tbs oil
3 minced shallots
3 minced garlic cloves
2 tsp cane sugar
1 cup chicken stock
1 tbs lemon juice
1 tsp hot chili sauce or paste

Grind nuts. Dice coconut cream. Heat oil. Sauté onions and garlic until translucent. Add remaining ingredients and simmer for 3 minutes.

Goes with: Poultry, pork, fish

Avocado Dip

2 ripe avocados
2 tbs lemon juice
1 clove garlic
2 chopped scallions
2 tbs sour cream
Salt and pepper
4 pinches cayenne pepper

Halve avocadoes lengthwise and remove pits. Remove fruit, mash with a fork and mix with lemon juice. Squeeze garlic through a press and add to avocadoes. Stir in remaining ingredients.

Goes with: Steak, poultry

Aioli

2 fresh egg yolks
1/2 tsp mustard
Salt
1 cup mild olive oil or sunflower oil
3 cloves garlic squeezed through a press
1/2 tsp lemon juice
Freshly ground pepper

Stir egg yolks, mustard and salt until creamy. Beat in oil, first drop by drop and then in a thin stream, but not too fast. Season with garlic, lemon juice and pepper.

Goes with: Fish, vegetables

10

Cocktail Sauce

Stir together 4 oz mayonnaise, 2 oz sour cream, $\frac{1}{2}$ tsp Hungarian sweet paprika, salt, pepper, 4 tbs ketchup, 3 pinches cayenne pepper, 1 tsp lemon juice and 1 tbs bottled horseradish

Goes with: Poultry, shrimp

Olive Butter

Combine 3 oz chopped black olives, 4 oz softened butter, salt, pepper, 2 pinches grated lemon zest and 2 garlic cloves squeezed through a press. Roll up tightly in plastic wrap and cover the plastic in foil before refrigerating or freezing.

Goes with: Lamb

Herb Butter

Combine 4 oz softened butter, 1 pinch grated lemon zest and $1\frac{1}{2}$ tbs freshly chopped herbs. Season to taste with salt and pepper. Roll up tightly in plastic wrap and cover the plastic in foil before refrigerating or freezing.

Goes with: Beef, pork, fish

Tuna Dip

Purée 1 can drained tuna, 8 oz crème fraîche, 2 tbs olive oil, salt, pepper, 1 tsp dijon mustard and 2 tbs lemon juice. Add 2 tbs capers to the puree.

Goes with: Poultry, vegetables

Green Sauce

Combine 3 tbs chopped parsley, 1 tbs chopped arugula, 1 chopped garlic clove, 6 tbs olive oil, 2 tbs sour cream, salt, pepper and 1 tbs lemon juice.

Goes with: Steaks, poultry and vegetables

Horseradish Cress Sauce

Combine 1 bunch watercress, 8 oz sour cream salt, pepper, 3 tsp bottled horseradish and $\frac{1}{2}$ tsp lemon juice.

Goes with: Fish

Classic Side Dishes

Grilled Corn on the Cob

Serves 4:
4 ears sweet corn
Salt and pepper
2 tbs corn oil

1 | Rinse corn, pat dry and precook in unsalted water uncovered for 15 minutes. Drain and pat dry.

2 | Rub corn on all sides with salt and pepper and brush with oil. Grill 10 minutes, turning occasionally.

Goes with: Steaks, poultry
Variation: Brush raw ears of corn with 2 oz softened butter or herb butter, wrap in aluminum foil and grill for about 40 minutes, turning occasionally. Season with salt and pepper.

Grilled Potatoes

Serves 4:
4 medium-sized, firm potatoes (about 6 oz each)
Salt and pepper
Oil for the foil

1 | Rinse potatoes. Pierce several times with a fork. Brush oil on 4 pieces of aluminum foil and wrap potatoes.

2 | Grill potatoes on the rack for 50 minutes, turning occasionally. Unwrap potatoes, split open and spoon directly out of the skin. Season with salt and pepper.

Goes with: Steaks, fish
Variation: Cook wrapped potatoes directly in the coals for about 35 minutes.

Garlic Bread

Serves 4–6:
2 cloves garlic
4 oz softened herb butter (recipe on page 11)
1 large baguette

1 | Peel garlic and squeeze through a press. Stir garlic into herb butter.

2 | Cut baguette only partway through into slices about I inch thick. Spread herb butter between slices. Wrap bread in aluminum foil and grill for 10 minutes, turning occasionally.

Goes with: Meat, fish, vegetables

Grilled Onions

Serves 4:
8 onions (2 oz each)
$2/3$ cup vegetable stock
3 tbs lemon juice
$4^1/_2$ tbs olive oil
Salt and pepper
2 tsp sugar

1 | Peel onions. Heat vegetable stock. Add onions, cover and precook for 20 minutes over low heat. Whisk together lemon juice, oil, salt and pepper.

2 | Drain onions and cut in half. Brush each half with 1 tbs marinade and sprinkle with a little sugar. Grill on the rack for 2 minutes on each side, then drizzle with remaining marinade.

Goes with: Steaks and poultry

Classic Side Dishes

Grilled Bell Peppers

Serves 4:
4 red bell peppers
Salt and pepper
. tbs balsamic vinegar
3 tbs olive oil

1 | Wash peppers and pat
dry. Grill whole peppers
or 15 minutes, turning
occasionally, until the
skin becomes black and
blistered. Cover peppers
with plastic wrap or a
moistened towel in a
metal mixing bowl for
0 minutes.

2 | Stir together salt, pep-
er, balsamic vinegar and
il. Peel the peppers with
our hands, cut in half,
emove seeds and cut into
ide strips. Drizzle with
marinade. Serve lukewarm
r cold.

Goes with: Poultry, fish

Tzatziki

Serves 4–6:
2 cups plain yogurt
1 tbs lemon juice
1 tbs olive oil
1 cucumber
2 cloves garlic
Salt and pepper

1 | Stir yogurt until creamy.
Stir in lemon juice and oil.
Peel cucumber, halve
lengthwise, remove seeds
and grate coarsely.

2 | Peel garlic, squeeze
through a press and add
to yogurt. Stir in cucumber.
Season to taste with lots
of salt and pepper.

Goes with: Fish skewers,
vegetables
Variation: Use 1½ cups
yogurt and ½ cup crème
fraîche.

Potato Salad
with Radishes

Serves 4:
2 pounds red potatoes
Salt and pepper
1 tsp dijon mustard
5 tbs vinegar
5 tbs oil
1 cup vegetable stock
1 bunch radishes
4 scallions
2 tbs chopped chives

1 | Rinse potatoes and
cook in salted water.
Whisk together salt, pep-
per, mustard, vinegar and
oil. Heat vegetable stock.
Drain potatoes, peel while
still hot and cut into thin
slices. Add stock and
dressing to the potatoes.
Marinate for 30 minutes.

2 | Rinse radishes, clean
and slice. Clean scallions,
rinse and chop. Combine
all ingredients.

Feta Tomatoes

Serves 4:
4 tomatoes
7 oz feta
Herb salt
2 tsp olive oil
4 small sprigs basil
Oil for the foil

1 | Rinse tomatoes, pat
dry and cut each into
6 slices. Cut feta into
16–20 slices. Grease 4
pieces of aluminum foil.
Arrange tomatoes and
feta on foil in alternating
layers. Season with
herb salt.

2 | Seal foil packets and
grill 10 minutes, turning
occasionally. Open pack-
ets, drizzle with
olive oil and sprinkle
with basil leaves.

Goes with: Grilled potatoes, steaks

13

Spicy Pork, Beef and Lamb

On warm summer evenings when the air starts to fill with the aroma of sizzling meat, thyme, rosemary and garlic, we know the next barbecue can't be far off. What a pleasure to be invited to a barbecue on one of those days! If you host your own barbecue, this chapter will not only provide you with a few classic favorites but will also give you many new ideas.

Quick Recipes

Lamb Chops with Thyme

SERVES 4:

➤ 2 cloves garlic
12 frenched lamb chops (4 oz each)
Salt | Freshly ground pepper
Thyme oil (page 9)

1 | Peel garlic and cut in half lengthwise. Rinse chops, pat dry, rub with garlic on both sides and season with salt and pepper.

2 | Brush chops with 2 tbs thyme oil and grill for 8 minutes, turning occasionally and brushing with remaining thyme oil.

Hamburgers

SERVES 4:

➤ 1 pound ground meat (beef or mixed)
Salt | Pepper | 4 pinches chili powder
2 tsp mustard | 1 tbs oil | 4 buns
4 rinsed lettuce leaves | 4 tomato slices
Ketchup and mustard (optional)

1 | Knead ground meat together with salt, pepper, chili powder and mustard. Shape into 4 flat hamburgers and brush with oil. Cut open buns.

2 | Grill hamburgers 4 minutes on each side. Toast buns briefly on the insides, then assemble all ingredients into hamburgers.

15

Hearty | Easy

Beer Marinated Pork Chops

SERVES 4:

➤ 1 clove garlic
4 tbs oil
1 tsp medium-hot mustard
4 tbs dark beer
$1/2$ tbs honey
Salt
Freshly ground pepper
1 tsp oregano
$1/2$ tsp Hungarian sweet paprika
4 pork chops (about 7 oz each)

⏱ Prep time: 20 minutes
⏱ Marinating time: 4 hours
⏱ Grilling time: 12 minutes
➤ Calories per serving: Approx 385

1 | Peel garlic and squeeze through a press. Combine garlic, oil, mustard, beer and honey. Season marinade with salt, pepper, oregano and paprika.

2 | Pat chops dry and brush liberally with marinade. Marinate meat in the refrigerator for 4 hours.

3 | Remove chops from marinade and drain excess marinade. Pour marinade that drains off into a cup. Grill chops 6 minutes on each side while brushing with marinade.

➤ Side dishes: Barbecue sauce (page 8), potato salad with radishes (page 13), farm bread whole-grain bread
➤ Drinks: light-colored beer (lager or pale ale)

Midwestern Specialty Classic

Barbecued Spare Ribs

SERVES 4:

➤ $4^1/4$ pounds spare ribs (pork ribs)
Barbecue sauce (double recipe, page 8)
2 oranges
2 cloves garlic
1 tbs brandy (optional)

⏱ Prep time: 30 minutes
⏱ Marinating time: 4 hours
⏱ Grilling time: 10 minutes
➤ Calories per serving: Approx 415

1 | Divide spare ribs into groups of about 3 ribs each and place in a large pot of boiling water. Cover and precook for 20 minutes over medium heat.

2 | Prepare barbecue sauce. Squeeze juice from oranges (yields about $3/4$ cup juice). Peel garlic and squeeze through a press. Stir garlic, juice and brandy into barbecue sauce. Drain ribs and cover with half the barbecue sauce while they're still hot. Cover and marinate in the refrigerator for 4 hours.

3 | Drain spare ribs from marinade and cut between ribs without cutting all the way through. Grill spare ribs 10 minutes while brushing with about 2 tbs barbecue sauce per 3-rib rack and turning occasionally. Serve remaining sauce on the side.

➤ Side dishes: Potato salad (page 13), grilled corn on the cob (page 12)
➤ Drinks: Lager or dry red wine

Photo bottom: **Beer Marinated Pork Chops**   *Photo top:* **Barbecued Spare Ribs** ➤

Fast | Hearty

Peppered Rump Steaks with Avocado Dip

SERVES 4:

➤ Avocado dip (page 10)

2 tbs black peppercorns

1 tbs allspice berries (or 1 tsp ground allspice)

4 rump steaks (about 7 oz each)

2 tbs oil

Salt

🕐 Prep time: 20 minutes

🕐 Grilling time: 6–12 minutes

➤ Calories per serving: Approx 740

1 | Prepare avocado dip. Coarsely crush pepper and allspice berries and spread out on a plate. Rinse rump steaks, pat dry and dredge in pepper mixture while pressing down firmly.

2 | Grill rump steaks 3–6 minutes on each side while brushing occasionally with oil. Season steaks with salt and serve with avocado dip.

➤ Side dishes: Grilled corn on the cob, grilled potatoes (page 12)

➤ Drinks: Red wine

Specialty of Argentina Hot

Center Cut Beef Tenderloin with Chimichurri Sauce

SERVES 4:

➤ Red wine marinade (page 9)

4 center cut beef tenderloin fillets (about 7 oz each)

1 red onion

1 large clove garlic

2 fresh red chili peppers

Salt | Freshly ground pepper

4 tbs lemon juice

4 tbs olive oil

2 tbs chopped Italian parsley

🕐 Prep time: 20 minutes

🕐 Marinating time: 4 hours

🕐 Grilling time: 6–12 minutes (see tip)

➤ Calories per serving: Approx 345

1 | Prepare marinade. Pat steaks dry. Set aside 2 tbs marinade. Pour remaining marinade over steaks. Cover and marinate in the refrigerator for 4 hours.

2 | For the chimichurri sauce, peel onion and dice finely. Peel garlic and squeeze through a press. Clean chili peppers, cut in half lengthwise, remove seeds, rinse and chop finely. Whisk together salt, pepper, chili peppers, garlic, lemon juice and oil. Stir in onion and parsley and let stand for 20 minutes.

3 | Remove steaks from marinade and pat dry. Grill 3–6 minutes on each side, turning occasionally and brushing with the marinade you set aside. Season steaks with salt and serve with sauce.

➤ Side dishes: Garlic bread, grilled potatoes (page 12), baguette

➤ Drinks: Dry red wine, lager or pale ale

TIP

Grilling Times

Grilling times for steaks are a matter of preference. Rare: 3 minutes on each side; medium: 4 minutes per side; well-done: 6 minutes per side.

Mediterranean | Can Prepare in Advance
Pork Tenderloin with Pesto

SERVES 4:

- 1 large bunch basil
- 2 cloves garlic
- 2 tbs pine nuts
- 2 tbs freshly grated Parmesan
- 5 tbs olive oil
- Salt
- Freshly ground pepper
- 2 pork tenderloins (about 11 oz each)
- 8 thin slices prosciutto
- Plus: Heavy-duty aluminum foil

- Prep time: 25 minutes
- Marinating time: 30 minutes
- Grilling time: 35 minutes
- Calories per serving: Approx 405

1 | For pesto, rinse basil, shake dry and pinch off leaves. Peel garlic and chop coarsely. Finely chop basil, garlic, pine nuts and Parmesan in a blender. Pour in 4 tbs olive oil and blend. Season to taste with salt and pepper.

2 | Brush oil onto the shiny side of two pieces of aluminum foil (about 12 x 18 inches). Rinse tenderloins, pat dry with paper towels and brush on all sides with pesto. Wrap 4 slices prosciutto around each pork fillet and then wrap each one in foil. Marinate meat in the refrigerator for 30 minutes.

3 | Grill pork tenderloins 35 minutes, turning occasionally. Then leave meat on the rack for 10 minutes where it isn't very hot. Unwrap tenderloins and slice diagonally.

- Side dishes: French bread, fig mustard cream (recipe at right)
- Drinks: A hearty red wine

TIPS

Fig Mustard Cream

A fig mustard cream is the perfect accompaniment to many pork dishes: Combine 4 oz Mascarpone, 1 tbs fig jam (may substitute apricot jam) and 3 tsp hot mustard. Season to taste with salt, pepper and 1 tsp lemon juice.

Quicker Recipe

If you don't have a lot of time, buy 5 oz of pesto in a jar instead of making your own.

If It Rains

If the weather is bad, you can prepare the pork tenderloins in the oven. Preheat the oven to 400°F. Place aluminum packets on the rack and cook tenderloins for 40 minutes. Let meat stand for 10 minutes before serving.

Specialty of Southern France | Can Prepare in Advance

Rosemary Lamb Chops with Olive Butter

SERVES 4:

- ➤ 4 double lamb chops (about 7 oz each)

  Salt

  Freshly ground pepper

  2 sprigs rosemary

  ½ cup olive oil

  Olive butter (page 11)

- ⏱ Prep time: 10 minutes
- ⏱ Marinating time: 2 hours
- ⏱ Grilling time: 10 minutes
- ➤ Calories per serving: Approx 1550

1 | Rinse lamb chops, pat dry and pound somewhat flat. Season meat with salt and pepper. Rinse rosemary and shake dry. Strip off needles and chop finely. Combine rosemary and oil. Brush chops with 5 tbs marinade and marinate in the refrigerator for 2 hours. Prepare olive butter.

2 | Grill lamb chops 5 minutes on each side, turning occasionally and brushing with remaining oil. Slice olive butter and arrange on top of meat.

- ➤ Side dishes: Baguette, tomato salad, green salad with mustard vinaigrette, grilled potatoes (page 12)
- ➤ Drinks: Red wine from France

Caribbean Specialty | Hot

Spicy Pork Steaks

SERVES 4:

- ➤ 1 scallion

  3 cloves garlic

  2 chili peppers

  1 piece fresh ginger (walnut-sized)

  Caribbean spice mixture (half recipe, page 8)

  2 tbs soy sauce

  3 tbs lemon juice

  2 tsp cane sugar (or sugar in the raw)

  Salt

  Freshly ground pepper

  4 pork loin steaks (about 6 oz each)

- ⏱ Prep time: 25 minutes
- ⏱ Marinating time. 4 hours
- ⏱ Grilling time: 12 minutes
- ➤ Calories per serving: Approx 240

1 | Clean scallion, rinse and chop coarsely. Peel garlic and chop coarsely. Clean chili peppers, cut in half lengthwise, remove seeds, rinse and cut into strips. Peel ginger and chop coarsely. Combine onion, garlic, chili peppers, spice mixture, soy sauce, lemon juice, cane sugar, salt and pepper in a blender and process into a thick seasoning sauce.

2 | Pat steaks dry, pound somewhat flat and brush with sauce. Marinate in the refrigerator for 4 hours. Drain meat, being careful to save the sauce. Grill 12 minutes, turning occasionally and brushing with seasoning sauce.

- ➤ Side dishes: Seasoned rice, tortilla chips
- ➤ Drinks: Fruity, semi-dry red wine

Light Poultry

Tender inside, crispy outside—this is the standard for the best poultry dishes all over the world. Barbecued poultry is prepared in households around the world, which is reflected in the diversity of these recipes. Whether it's rosemary chicken from the Mediterranean or crispy honey-crusted chicken wings from right here in the US, you can create a summer holiday spirit, even in your own backyard.

Quick Recipes

Turkey Rolls with Serrano Ham

SERVES 4:

➤ 8 small, thin turkey cutlets (2 oz each)
Salt | Pepper
2 tsp dijon or whole-grain mustard
8 thin slices serrano ham (or prosciutto)
8 soft, dried apricots | 1 tbs olive oil
8 metal skewers

1 | Pat cutlets dry and pound flat. Season with salt and pepper. Coat one side with mustard. Cut ham slices in half. Arrange ham and apricots on top of mustard.

2 | Roll up fillets and secure with skewers. Brush rolls with oil and grill 10 minutes, turning occasionally.

Sherry Chicken Breast

SERVES 4:

➤ Sherry marinade (page 9)
4 skinless chicken breast fillets (about 6 oz each) | Salt | Pepper

1 | Prepare marinade. Rinse fillets, pat dry and pound somewhat flat. Season meat with salt and pepper and brush on all sides with marinade. Marinate in the refrigerator for at least 15 minutes.

2 | Grill chicken fillets 10 minutes, turning occasionally.

Traditional | Hearty
Spit-Roasted Rosemary Chicken

SERVES 4:
- ➤ 6 sprigs rosemary
- 2 cloves garlic
- 2 chickens
  (2¹/₂ pounds each)
- Salt
- Freshly ground pepper
- 8 tbs oil
- ¹/₄ tsp Hungarian
  hot paprika
- ¹/₂ tsp Hungarian
  sweet paprika
- 1 tbs tomato paste
- 1 tbs lemon juice

- ⏲ Prep time: 20 minutes
- ⏲ Marinating time: 1 hour
- ⏲ Grilling time: 1 hour
- ➤ Calories per serving:
  Approx 975

1 | Rinse rosemary and shake dry. Strip needles off of 2 sprigs and chop finely. Peel garlic cloves and cut into quarters. Rinse chickens, pat dry and rub inside and out with salt and pepper. Place 2 sprigs rosemary and 2 quarter garlic cloves inside the cavity of each chicken. Tie chickens with butcher's twine so the wings and legs stay close to the body.

2 | Whisk together oil, paprika, tomato paste, lemon juice and chopped rosemary to form a marinade. Brush chickens with half the marinade and marinate in the refrigerator for approx 1 hour.

3 | Drain chickens, thread onto the spit and secure. Grill chickens 1 hour while turning constantly, occasionally brushing with remaining half of marinade.

- ➤ Side dishes: Potato salad (page 13), soft pretzels

TIP | **Without the Spit**
If you don't have a rotisserie, cut the chickens in half, season with salt and pepper and brush with marinade. Grill halves 20 minutes with the skin side up, turn and grill another 25 minutes.

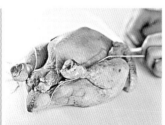

1 Secure string
Tie string around one leg.

2 Close
Bring string under the rump and tie to the other leg.

3 Marinate
Brush chicken with marinade.

27

Americana
Can Prepare in Advance

Honey-Crusted Chicken Wings

SERVES 4:

- ➤ 20 chicken wings
  (3 to 3$\frac{1}{2}$ pounds total)
  Salt
  Freshly ground pepper
  5 tbs ketchup
  5 tbs soy sauce
  $\frac{1}{2}$ tbs mustard
  1 tsp chili powder
  5 tbs oil
  1$\frac{1}{2}$ tbs honey

🕑Prep time: 20 minutes
🕑Marinating time: 4 hours
🕑Grilling time: 20 minutes
➤ Calories per serving:
  Approx 590

1 | Rinse chicken wings, pat dry and cut off tips if necessary. Rub with salt and pepper. Whisk together ketchup, soy sauce, mustard, chili powder and 3 tbs oil. Set aside 5 tbs of marinade. Brush wings with remaining marinade. Cover and marinate in the refrigerator for 4 hours.

2 | Grill chicken for about 15 minutes, turning occasionally and brushing with 2$\frac{1}{2}$ tbs of the marinade you set aside. Stir honey and remaining oil into marinade. Brush onto wings and grill another 5 minutes, turning frequently.

➤ Side dishes: Barbecue sauce (page 8), peanut sauce (page 10)
➤ Drinks: Beer

Exotic | Hot

Caribbean Chicken

SERVES 4:

- ➤ 1 lime
  7 allspice berries
  (or $\frac{1}{2}$ tsp ground allspice)
  1 clove garlic
  2 tbs hot chili sauce
  2 tsp cane sugar
  (or sugar in the raw)
  8 tbs oil
  Salt
  Freshly ground pepper
  1 chicken (about 4 pounds)
  Oil for the grill pan

🕑 Prep time: 25 minutes
🕑 Marinating time: 2 hours
🕑 Grilling time: 30 minutes
➤ Calories per serving:
  Approx 760

1 | Rinse lime and dry. Finely grate off zest and squeeze out juice. Crush allspice in a mortar. Peel garlic and squeeze through a press. Whisk together garlic, chili sauce, cane sugar and oil. Season with salt, pepper, allspice, lime juice and lime zest.

2 | Rinse chicken, pat dry and cut into 8 pieces with a cleaver or sharp kitchen knife. Season with salt and pepper. Set aside 3 tbs of marinade. Brush chicken with remaining marinade and marinate in the refrigerator for 2 hours.

3 | Place chicken in greased grill pan. Grill 30 minutes, turning occasionally and brushing with the marinade you set aside.

➤ Side dishes: Grilled corn on the cob (page 12), chili sauce
➤ Drinks: Lager or pale ale

Specialty of India
Easy

Tandoori Chicken

SERVES 4:

➤ 4 skinless chicken breast fillets (5–6 oz each)

2 tbs lemon juice

12 oz yogurt (3.5% fat)

1 piece fresh ginger (walnut-sized)

3 cloves garlic

1/2 tsp ground cumin

1/4 tsp ground coriander

Freshly ground black pepper

1 tbs hot curry

Oil for the grill pan

🕐 Prep time: 30 minutes
🕐 Marinating time: 4 hours
🕐 Grilling time. 30 minutes
➤ Calories per serving: Approx 220

1 | Rinse chicken breast fillets and pat dry. Cut each fillet in half crosswise. Score meat several times about 1/4 inch deep, rub with salt and 1 tbs lemon juice and set aside.

2 | Stir yogurt until creamy. Peel ginger and grate finely.

Peel garlic and squeeze through a press. Combine yogurt, ginger, garlic, remaining lemon juice and spices. Set aside 2 tbs of marinade. Coat chicken with remaining marinade and marinate for 4 hours.

3 | Drain chicken well and grill 30 minutes in greased grill pan. Turn once and brush with remaining marinade.

➤ Side dishes: Naan bread, rice, chutney

For Company | Traditional

Glazed Duck Breast

SERVES 4:

➤ 2 duck breast fillets (10 oz each)

Salt

Freshly ground pepper

1 piece fresh ginger (walnut-sized)

2 tbs dry sherry

2 tbs soy sauce

2 tbs orange liqueur

3 pinches cayenne pepper

2 tbs oil

Oil for the grill pan

2 tsp balsamic vinegar

2 tbs apricot jam

🕐 Prep time: 25 minutes
🕐 Marinating time: 4 hours
🕐 Grilling time: 20 minutes
➤ Calories per serving: Approx 420

1 | Score duck skin in a diamond pattern and season with salt and pepper. Peel ginger, grate and stir together with sherry, soy sauce, liqueur and cayenne pepper. Brush fillets with marinade, place in the marinade with the skin side up for 4 hours.

2 | Drain fillets. Brush 1 tbs oil onto meat side and place in greased grill pan with the skin side down. Grill ten minutes, turn and grill another 6 minutes. Combine balsamic vinegar, jam and remaining oil. Brush onto fillets and grill 2 minutes on each side directly on the grill rack until crispy.

➤ Side dishes: Chili sauce, basmati rice, baguette

Photo bottom: **Glazed Duck Breast**   Photo top: **Tandoori Chicken** ➤

Elegant Fish

Grilled fish may not be an everyday meal, but it's a culinary delight and a great option when you want to serve your guests something special. Even pampered gourmets will appreciate grilled salmon, swordfish and red snapper. Remember one thing: Only fish and fish fillets that have firm meat are suitable for the grill.

Quick Recipes

Rockfish with Lime Butter

SERVES 4:
- ➤ 4 oz softened butter
  Salt | Freshly ground pepper
  $1/4$ tsp grated lime zest
  $1/2$ tsp lime juice | 1 tbs chopped chives
  4 rockfish fillets (7 oz each)
  Oil for the grill pans

1 | Combine butter, salt, pepper and lime zest. Set aside 1 tbs of this butter mixture. Stir lime juice and chives into remaining butter. Roll up tightly in plastic wrap and cover the plastic in foil before refrigerating or freezing.

2 | Brush softened butter you set aside onto fillets. Grill 6 minutes on each side in greased grill pans. Serve with lime butter.

Monkfish with Olive Caper Sauce

SERVES 4:
- ➤ 8 pitted kalamata olives
  1 tbs drained capers
  Salt | Freshly ground pepper
  2 pinches grated lemon zest
  $1/2$ tsp dijon mustard
  2 tbs lemon juice | 5 tbs olive oil
  4 slices monkfish (about 6 oz each)

1 | Chop olives and capers. Combine both with salt, pepper, lemon zest, mustard, lemon juice and 4 tbs oil.

2 | Brush remaining oil onto fish and grill on the rack for about 4 minutes on each side. Season with salt and pepper and serve with sauce.

Fruity

Hawaiian Style Red Snapper

SERVES 4:

- ➤ 2 pounds red snapper fillets with skin (may substitute orange roughy or rockfish fillets)

  2½ tbs lime juice

  2 tbs olive oil

  1 shallot

  2 cloves garlic

  14 oz tomatoes

  2 tbs mango chutney

  2 tbs white wine vinegar

  Several dashes of Tabasco

  Salt

  Freshly ground pepper

- ⏱ Prep time: 20 minutes
- ⏱ Marinating time: 30 minutes
- ⏱ Grilling time: 8 minutes
- ➤ Calories per serving: Approx 285

1 | Rinse fish and pat dry. Combine 2 tbs lime juice and oil and brush onto fillets. Marinate in the refrigerator for 30 minutes.

2 | Peel shallot and chop. Peel garlic and mince. Pour boiling water over tomatoes, peel and dice finely. Combine tomatoes, shallot, garlic, mango chutney and vinegar and heat. Simmer uncovered for 10 minutes over low heat. Let cool and season to taste with Tabasco, salt and remaining lime juice.

3 | Pat fish fillets dry and grill 3–4 minutes on each side. Season with salt and pepper. Serve fillets with tomato mango sauce.

- ➤ Side dishes: Aromatic rice, iceberg lettuce salad

Hot | Asian

Ginger Shrimp

SERVES 4:

- ➤ 2 tbs lemon juice

  4 tbs oil

  1 tsp freshly grated ginger

  4 pinches cayenne pepper

  Salt

  Freshly ground pepper

  20 unpeeled, raw jumbo shrimp (about 1½ pounds)

  1 scallion

  ½ bunch cilantro (may substitute Italian parsley)

  ½ cup sweet chili sauce

- ⏱ Prep time: 25 minutes
- ⏱ Marinating time: 1 hour
- ⏱ Grilling time: 6 minutes
- ➤ Calories per serving: Approx 190

1 | Stir together lemon juice and oil. Season to taste with ginger, cayenne, salt and pepper. Peel shrimp except for the tail and devein. Brush with marinade and marinate in the refrigerator for 1 hour.

2 | Clean scallion, rinse and chop finely. Rinse cilantro, shake dry and chop finely. Stir cilantro and scallion into chili sauce.

3 | Grill shrimp 3 minutes on each side. Serve with chili sauce.

- ➤ Side dishes: Basmati rice, shrimp chips
- ➤ Drinks: Semi-dry white wine

Photo bottom: **Ginger Shrimp**   *Photo top:* **Hawaiian Style Red Snapper** ➤

Easy | For Company

Stuffed Herb Trout

SERVES 4:

➤ 1 onion

3 cloves garlic

1 bunch Italian parsley

3 tbs oil

2 tbs dry white wine

Salt and pepper

4 cleaned trout
(about 10 oz each)

1 lemon

○ Prep time: 25 minutes

○ Grilling time: 10 minutes

➤ Calories per serving:
Approx 230

1 | Peel and dice onion. Peel garlic and mince. Rinse parsley, shake dry and chop finely. Heat 1 tbs oil in a pan and sauté onion and garlic until translucent. Add wine and bring to a boil. Let cool. Season with parsley, salt and pepper.

2 | Rinse trout inside and out with cold water and pat dry with paper towels. Rub inside and out with salt and pepper. Stuff fish with onion mixture. Brush remaining oil onto both sides. Rinse lemon, dry and cut into quarters.

3 | Grill trout 5 minutes on each side. Serve with lemon quarters.

➤ Side dishes: Grilled potatoes (page 12) or boiled potatoes, herb butter (page 11), green salad, carrot salad

➤ Drinks: Dry white wine

➤ Variation:

Mackerel

Instead of trout, use whole, cleaned mackerel.

TIPS

Grilling Whole Fish

Grill each fish separately in a special grill basket for fish, or grill several at a time in a hinged grill basket. If you don't have either of these tools, grill the fish on the greased rack and turn it carefully using a long metal spatula.

If It Rains

If it rains, you'll have no trouble preparing fish in the oven. Preheat the oven broiler and place the fish on the broiler rack on top of a drip pan. Broil the fish on the center shelf for 5–6 minutes on each side.

Specialty of Spain
Fast

Grilled Red Mullet

SERVES 4:

- ➤ 4 small sprigs rosemary
  4 sprigs thyme
  4 cleaned red mullet (about 9 oz each)
  Salt
  4 tbs olive oil
  4 lemon wedges

⏱ Prep time: 10 minutes
⏱ Grilling time: 10 minutes
➤ Calories per serving: Approx 240

1 | Rinse rosemary and thyme and shake dry. Rinse red mullet and pat dry. Salt fish inside and out and place 1 sprig rosemary and 1 sprig thyme inside the cavity of each fish. Brush outside with oil.

2 | Grill fish for about 5 minutes on each side. Serve red mullet with lemon wedges.

➤ Side dishes: Aioli (page 10), white bread, grilled bell peppers (page 13)
➤ Drinks: Dry white wine

TIP

Instant Aioli

If you don't have time to make fresh aioli, substitute 10 oz of prepared mayonnaise and season to taste with a little lemon juice and 2–3 garlic cloves squeezed through a press.

Exotic | Fast

Salmon Steaks with Papaya Bell-Pepper Salsa

SERVES 4:

- ➤ 5 tbs lemon juice
  Grated zest from ¼ lemon
  1½ tbs olive oil
  4 salmon steaks (about 7 oz each)
  3 scallions
  2 small papaya (8 oz each)
  1 small red bell pepper (4 oz)
  1 tbs Italian parsley
  Salt and pepper
  Cayenne pepper

⏱ Prep time: 20 minutes
⏱ Grilling time: 10 minutes
➤ Calories per serving: Approx 480

1 | Combine 1 tbs lemon juice, lemon zest and olive oil. Rinse salmon steaks, pat dry and brush with marinade. Refrigerate for 15 minutes.

2 | Clean scallions, wash and chop finely. Peel papaya, cut in half, remove seeds and dice fruit finely. Cut bell pepper in half, remove seeds, rinse and dice finely. Combine scallions, papaya, bell pepper, parsley and remaining lemon juice. Season with salt, pepper and cayenne.

3 | Grill salmon steaks 5 minutes on each side. Season with salt and pepper. Serve with papaya bell-pepper salsa.

➤ Side dishes: Baguette, spicy rice salad, grilled onions (page 12)
➤ Drinks: Dry white wine, lager or pale ale

Caribbean Specialty
Hot

Tuna Steaks with Fiery Tomato Sauce

SERVES 4:

➤ 2 tbs oil

4 tbs lime juice

3 pinches ground coriander

Freshly ground pepper

4 tuna steaks (7 oz each)

1¼ pounds tomatoes

2 small red chili peppers

1 large clove garlic

3 scallions

Salt

1 pinch sugar

🕐 Prep time: 25 minutes

🕐 Marinating time: 30 minutes

🕐 Grilling time: 8 minutes

➤ Calories per serving:
Approx 520

1 | Combine oil, 1 tbs lime juice, coriander and pepper. Rinse tuna, pat dry and brush with marinade. Marinate in the refrigerator for 30 minutes.

2 | Pour boiling water over tomatoes, peel, remove cores and dice finely. Clean chili peppers, cut in half lengthwise, remove seeds, rinse and chop finely. Peel garlic and squeeze through a press. Clean scallions, rinse and chop finely. Combine tomatoes, chili peppers, scallions and garlic. Season to taste with salt, pepper, sugar and remaining lime juice.

3 | Grill tuna steaks 4 minutes on each side. Serve with tomato sauce.

➤ Side dishes: Rice, tortilla chips

Mediterranean
Can Prepare in Advance

Swordfish with Melon Salsa

SERVES 4:

➤ 4 slices swordfish
(about 7 oz each)

Lemon marinade (page 9)

14 oz watermelon
(preferably seedless)

½ cucumber (about 6 oz)

2 shallots

2 cloves garlic

½ bunch basil

4 tbs lemon juice

Salt and pepper

Cayenne pepper

🕐 Prep time: 20 minutes

🕐 Marinating time: 30 minutes

🕐 Grilling time: 8 minutes

➤ Calories per serving:
Approx 280

1 | Brush fish with marinade and refrigerate for 30 minutes. Peel melon, remove seeds and cut fruit into small cubes. Rinse cucumber, cut in half lengthwise, remove seeds and dice finely. Peel shallots and chop finely. Peel garlic and squeeze through a press.

2 | Rinse basil and chop finely. Combine melon, cucumber, shallots, garlic, basil and lemon juice. Season with salt, pepper and cayenne.

3 | Grill fish 4 minutes on each side. Season with salt and pepper. Serve with melon salsa.

➤ Side dishes: Baguette, grissini

➤ Drinks: White burgundy

Vegetarian Delights

Everybody's had grilled potatoes or carmelized onions as a side dish with steak. In this chapter, the focus is the vegetables, potatoes, and cheese, which can be used to prepare dishes that may surprise you. Timid souls who think the grill is only for meat and fish can start by preparing half recipes and serving them as appetizers.

Quick Recipes

Crispy Pumpkin Wedges

SERVES 4:

➤ 2¹/₄ pounds pumpkin | 6 tbs olive oil
  1 clove garlic squeezed through a press
  Salt | Pepper | ¹/₄ tsp ground allspice
  2 tsp cane sugar (or sugar in the raw)
  2 tsp balsamic vinegar

1 | Remove seeds from pumpkin and cut into wedges about ¹/₂ inch wide. Brush with 1 tbs oil. Whisk together remaining ingredients.

2 | Grill wedges 7 minutes on each side. Brush with seasoning oil and grill 1 additional minute on each side until crispy. Goes well with herb butter.

Grilled Tomatoes with Mozzarella

SERVES 4:

➤ 8 vine-ripened or hothouse tomatoes
  2 drained Mozzarella balls (4 oz each)
  Salt | Pepper | 3 tbs olive oil
  Several basil leaves
  Oil for grill the pan

1 | Rinse tomatoes, pat dry and cut in half crosswise. Cut Mozzarella balls into 16 slices.

2 | Grill tomatoes for 8 minutes in a greased grill pan with the cut sides down. Turn, top with Mozzarella and grill another 5 minutes. Season with salt and pepper. Drizzle with olive oil and garnish with basil.

Mediterranean
Can Prepare in Advance

Potatoes with Smoked Gouda and Tomatoes

SERVES 4:

- ➤ 8 medium-sized, firm potatoes
  3 tomatoes
  Salt
  Freshly ground pepper
  1½ tsp oregano
  10 oz smoked gouda
  Oil for the foil
  16 toothpicks

- ⏲ Prep time: 30 minutes
- ⏲ Grilling time: 15 minutes
- ➤ Calories per serving: Approx 240

1 | Rinse potatoes and cook with peels in salted boiling water. Let cool. Rinse tomatoes, pat dry and cut into 16 slices. Sprinkle tomatoes with salt, pepper and oregano.

2 | Cut cheese into 16 slices and cut each slice in half. Grease 8 pieces of aluminum foil. Cut potatoes lengthwise into 3 slices each and layer each potato as follows: Bottom potato slice, cheese, tomato, cheese, middle potato slice, cheese, tomato, cheese, top potato slice. Secure with toothpicks from each side to make sure everything holds together.

3 | Wrap potatoes in foil. Grill 15 minutes, turning once.

- ➤ Side dishes: Olive butter (recipe on page 11) or marinated olives
- ➤ Drinks: Hearty red wine

Middle-Eastern
Inexpensive

Veggie Burgers

SERVES 4:

- ➤ 2 cans garbanzo beans (16 oz each)
  3 tbs sesame seeds
  1 large onion
  2 cloves garlic
  1 tbs dijon mustard
  Salt
  Freshly ground pepper
  2 tsp ground cumin
  4 pinches cayenne pepper
  2 oz breadcrumbs
  2 tbs oil

- ⏲ Prep time: 25 minutes
- ⏲ Grilling time: 8 minutes
- ➤ Calories per serving: Approx 560

1 | Drain garbanzo beans in a colander. Toast sesame seeds in a pan without oil. Peel onion and dice. Peel garlic and chop.

2 | Purée garbanzo beans, sesame seeds, onion and garlic in a blender. Season heavily with mustard, salt, pepper, cumin and cayenne. Work breadcrumbs into the mixture.

3 | Form mixture into 8 burgers and brush on all sides with oil. Grill veggie burgers about 4 minutes on each side.

- ➤ Side dishes: Flatbread, sandwich buns, tzatziki (page 13), green sauce (page 11), chili sauce

For Company | Easy
Tomatoes with Goat Cheese and Arugula

SERVES 4:

➤ **4 beefsteak tomatoes (8 oz each)**
Salt
Freshly ground pepper
4 slices white bread (about 1 oz each)
2 cloves garlic
4 tbs olive oil
6 oz firm goat cheese
¹/₂ bunch arugula
Oil for the aluminum foil

🕐 Prep time: 30 minutes
🕐 Grilling time: 20 minutes
➤ Calories per serving: Approx 290

1 | Rinse tomatoes and dry. Cut off tops and set aside for lids. Hollow out tomatoes. Season inside with salt and pepper. Turn tomatoes upside-down and let drain.

2 | Remove crust from bread and cut into cubes. Peel garlic and mince. Heat oil in a pan and sauté bread cubes until crispy. Add garlic and sauté briefly.

3 | Finely dice goat cheese. Rinse arugula, clean, shake dry and chop finely. Combine cheese, arugula and bread mixture. Season with salt and pepper. Grease 4 pieces of foil.

4 | Fill tomatoes with mixture and set lids on top. Wrap in foil and grill 20 minutes, turning occasionally.

➤ Side dishes: Green salad with mustard vinaigrette
➤ Drinks: Dry rosé or red wine

Fruity | For Company
Bananas and Honey

SERVES 4:

➤ **2 oz softened butter**
2 tbs vanilla
1 tsp sugar
4 pinches cinnamon
1 dash lemon juice
4 bananas
4 tsp clover honey

🕐 Prep time: 30 minutes
🕐 Grilling time: 10 minutes
➤ Calories per serving: Approx 195

1 | Stir butter until creamy. Stir in vanilla, sugar, cinnamon and lemon juice and refrigerate.

2 | Place bananas on the rack in their peels and grill 10 minutes, turning occasionally.

3 | Cut through peels lengthwise and carefully open up. Serve bananas with cinnamon butter and honey.

➤ Side dish: Coconut cookies

TIP

Banana Flambé
Heat 8 tbs strong, dark rum in a ladle. Light rum and pour over bananas.

Mediterranean | Hearty
Sliced Eggplant with Olives and Feta

SERVES 4:

- ½ bunch thyme
- 4 tbs lemon juice
- 5 tbs olive oil
- Salt
- Freshly ground black pepper
- 2 eggplant (about 10 oz each)
- 1 bunch Italian parsley
- 2 oz pitted black olives, marinated in herbs
- 6 oz feta cheese
- 3 tbs yogurt
- Oil for the grill pan

- ⏱ Prep time: 35 minutes
- ⏱ Marinating time: 2 hours
- ⏱ Grilling time: 15 minutes
- ➤ Calories per serving: Approx 240

1 | Rinse thyme, shake dry, chop leaves finely and combine with lemon juice, oil, salt and pepper. Rinse eggplant, pat dry and slice crosswise into a total of 40 slices. Brush eggplant slices with marinade and let stand 2 hours.

2 | Rinse parsley, shake dry and chop finely. Coarsely chop olives. Mash feta and combine with yogurt, olives, parsley and pepper.

3 | Drain eggplant. Spread cheese mixture on 20 slices and top with remaining slices, pressing down gently. Grill 15 minutes in a greased grill pan, turning occasionally.

- ➤ Side dishes: Flatbread, tzatziki (page 13)
- ➤ Drinks: Dry white wine

Fast | For Company
Grilled Radicchio with Gorgonzola Cream

SERVES 4:

- ➤ 10 oz Gorgonzola
- 10 oz sour cream
- 2 tsp lemon juice
- Salt
- Freshly ground pepper
- 2 tbs chopped parsley
- 4 large, firm heads of radicchio
- 12 tbs olive oil

- ⏱ Prep time: 20 minutes
- ⏱ Grilling time: About 8 minutes
- ➤ Calories per serving: Approx 600

1 | Combine Gorgonzola, sour cream and lemon juice and stir with a hand blender or fork until smooth and creamy. Add salt, pepper and parsley.

2 | Rinse radicchio, clean, pat dry and cut in half lengthwise. Combine oil with salt and pepper. Brush radicchio with oil outside and between leaves and grill 4 minutes on each side, occasionally pressing radicchio down onto the rack with a spatula. Serve with Gorgonzola cream. *Variation:* Radicchio can also be wrapped in prosciutto prior to grilling.

- ➤ Side dishes: Italian breadsticks
- ➤ Drinks: very dry white wine

TIP

Radicchio di Treviso
This oblong radicchio is also excellent for grilling.

Skewers for a Change

Whether it's meat, fish or vegetables, once you marinate and skewer food for the grill, it becomes a feast for the eyes and the taste buds. Although they take a little more time to assemble, skewers are easier to turn once on the grill. You can use the traditional wooden or metal skewers, which are no more than 8 inches long, or the longer metal skewers that are usually about 12 inches long.

Quick Recipes

Sausage Skewers with Spicy Ketchup

SERVES 4:

➤ 10 pork sausages (1¼ pound total)
4 small onions (8 oz total)
⅔ cup ketchup | 2 tsp mustard
1 tsp Hungarian sweet paprika
8 skewers

1 | Cut sausages into bite-sized pieces. Peel onions and cut into quarters. Alternately thread the two ingredients onto skewers. Combine ketchup, mustard and paprika to form a sauce.

2 | Grill skewers 8 minutes, turning occasionally. After 6 minutes, brush with 3 tbs sauce. Serve with remaining sauce.

Bread and Cheese Skewers

SERVES 4:

➤ 10 oz French bread
8 oz cheese (e.g. Manchego, Gruyère)
16 cherry tomatoes | 4 tbs olive oil
Oil for the grill pans | 8 skewers

1 | Cut bread and cheese into cubes of about 1 inch. Rinse tomatoes and pat dry. Thread bread, cheese and tomatoes onto skewers. Brush with 2 tbs oil.

2 | Grill skewers 8 minutes in a greased grill pan, turning occasionally. Arrange skewers on a serving dish and sprinkle with remaining olive oil.

Greek | For Company

Fish Kebabs with Zucchini

SERVES 4:

- ➤ 4 small zucchini (14 oz total)

  1¼ pounds tuna fillet

  Lemon marinade (page 9)

  8 fresh bay leaves

  Salt and pepper

  4 long skewers

  Oil for the grill pans

- ⏲ Prep time: 25 minutes
- ⏲ Marinating time: 30 minutes
- ⏲ Grilling time: About 12 minutes
- ➤ Calories per serving: Approx 360

1 | Rinse zucchini, pat dry and cut into ½ inch slices. Pat fish fillets dry and cut into cubes of no more than 1 inch.

2 | Stir fish and zucchini into marinade. Cover and marinate in the refrigerator for 30 minutes. Drain in a colander, being careful to save the marinade. Alternately thread fish, zucchini and bay leaves onto the skewers.

3 | Grill skewers 10 minutes in greased grill pans, occasionally turning and brushing with marinade. Then grill 2 minutes directly on the rack until crispy on all sides. Season with salt and pepper.

- ➤ Side dishes: White bread, aioli (page 10), horseradish cress sauce (page 11)
- ➤ Drinks: Dry white wine

Specialty of Thailand
Hot

Chicken Satay Skewers

SERVES 4:

- ➤ 1 piece fresh ginger (walnut-sized)

  1 tsp hot curry powder

  2 tbs soy sauce

  1 tbs lime juice (may substitute lemon juice)

  1 tsp cane sugar (or sugar in the raw)

  2 tbs oil

  1¼ pounds skinless chicken breast fillets

  Peanut sauce (page 10)

  Salt

  Freshly ground pepper

  12 skewers

- ⏲ Prep time: 30 minutes
- ⏲ Marinating time: 2 hours
- ⏲ Grilling time: 8 minutes
- ➤ Calories per serving: Approx 500

1 | Peel ginger and grate finely. Combine ginger, curry, soy sauce, lime juice, cane sugar and oil. Rinse chicken fillets, pat dry and cut into strips ¼ inch wide. Stir meat into marinade and marinate in the refrigerator for at least 2 hours.

2 | Prepare peanut sauce. Drain meat and thread onto skewers in accordion fashion. Grill skewers 8 minutes, turning often. Season meat with salt and pepper. Serve with peanut sauce.

- ➤ Side dishes: Rice, cucumber salad

Photo bottom: **Fish Kebabs with Zucchini**   *Photo top:* **Chicken Satay Skewers** ➤

Mediterranean | Inexpensive

Provençal Vegetable Skewers

SERVES 4:

➤ 16 mushrooms
1 yellow bell pepper
2 small zucchini
2 small onions
16 cherry tomatoes
5 sprigs thyme
1 sprig rosemary
8 tbs olive oil
Salt
Freshly ground pepper
2 tsp herbes de Provence
(in herb section of
supermarket)
8 skewers

🕒 Prep time: 30 minutes
🕒 Marinating time: 1 hour
🕒 Grilling time: 15 minutes
➤ Calories per serving:
Approx 215

1 | Clean mushrooms with paper towels and cut off end of stalks. Rinse bell pepper, cut in half, clean, cut in half again and then crosswise into wide strips. Rinse zucchini, clean and cut into bite-sized pieces. Peel onions and cut into quarters. Rinse tomatoes and dry with paper towels.

2 | Rinse thyme and rosemary and shake dry. Strip leaves and needles from stems and chop finely. Combine olive oil, salt, pepper, herbes de Provence, thyme and rosemary.

3 | Set aside 2 tbs of seasoned oil. Place vegetables, onions and mushrooms in a bowl and pour remaining oil over the top. Shake the bowl around until all the vegetables are coated. Marinate for 1 hour.

4 | Alternately thread vegetables onto skewers. Grill skewers 15 minutes, turning occasionally and brushing with remaining oil.

➤ Side dishes: Baguette, green sauce (page 11), aioli (page 10), olive butter (page 11)
➤ Drinks: Dry rosé, hearty red wine

TIPS

Rosemary Skewers

If you have a garden where rosemary thrives, cut off 8 sturdy stalks and strip off the needles up to the very tip. Using a knife, carve the stalks to a point just below the first branches. Thread vegetables onto these rosemary stalks.

For Garlic Lovers

Peel 1 clove garlic, squeeze through a press and add to the seasoning oil.

Specialty of Greece
Hearty

Meatballs and Bell Peppers

SERVES 4:

- 1 onion
  1 clove garlic
  1 bunch parsley
  4 oz feta
  2 green bell peppers
  1¼ pounds ground beef
  2 tbs low-fat quark
  Salt
  Freshly ground pepper
  ½ tsp mustard
  2 tbs freshly grated Parmesan
  1 tbs olive oil
  4 long skewers

- Prep time: 35 minutes
- Grilling time: 15 minutes
- Calories per serving: Approx 520

1 | Peel onion and dice finely. Peel garlic and mince. Rinse parsley, shake dry and chop. Cut feta into 24 small cubes. Rinse bell peppers, cut in half, clean and cut each half into 6 pieces.

2 | Mix together ground meat, quark, salt, pepper, mustard, parsley, onion, garlic and Parmesan. Wrap each feta cube in the meat mixture and shape into a ball.

3 | Alternately thread meatballs and bell pepper pieces onto skewers and brush with oil. Grill skewers 15 minutes, turning occasionally.

- Side dishes: Flatbread, tzatziki (page 13), marinated olives
- Drinks: Dry white wine

Middle-Eastern
Can Prepare in Advance

Turkey Kebab

SERVES 4:

- ½ onion
  1 lemon
  1 tsp dried thyme
  1 tsp dried oregano
  ¼ tsp cinnamon
  1 tsp tomato paste
  8 tbs olive oil
  Salt | Black pepper
  1¼ pounds turkey breast fillets
  2 small red onions
  4 long skewers

- Prep time: 25 minutes
- Marinating time: 4 hours
- Grilling time: 15 minutes
- Calories per serving: Approx 345

1 | Mince onion. Grate off lemon zest and squeeze out juice. Combine onion, thyme, oregano, cinnamon, tomato paste, oil, salt, pepper, lemon juice and zest.

2 | Cut turkey breast into cubes, stir into marinade and marinate for 4 hours.

3 | Peel red onions and cut each into 10 wedges. Drain meat in a colander and brush onions with drained-off marinade. Alternately thread meat and onions onto skewers and grill 15 minutes, turning occasionally.

- Side dishes: Tzatziki (page 13), flatbread

TIP

Lamb Version
Instead of turkey breast, use leg of lamb.

BBQ Party Ideas

Mediterranean Feast

For 8 people:

Grilled Tomatoes with Mozzarella
(page 43, 4 servings)

Monkfish with Olive Caper Sauce
(page 33, 8 servings)

Pork Tenderloin with Pesto (page 21, 4 servings)

Rosemary Lamb Chops with Olive Butter
(page 22, 4 servings)

Provençal Vegetable Skewers (page 55, 4 servings)

Aperitif

Bellini

Makes 8 glasses: Pour boiling water over
2 aromatic peaches, let peaches steep briefly
and then rinse under cold water. Peel peaches,
remove pits and purée. Add 4 tbs peach liqueur
and $1/2$ tsp lemon juice. Pour peach purée into
glasses and add about 3 cups chilled sparkling
white wine. Serve immediately.

Caribbean Fiesta

Pumpkin Wedges (page 43, 4 servings)

Avocado Dip (page 10, 8 servings)

Ginger Shrimp (page 34, 4 servings)

Salmon Steaks with Papaya Bell-Pepper Sauce
(page 38, 8 servings)

Spicy Pork Steaks (page 22, 4 servings)

Caribbean Chicken (page 28, 4 servings)

Aperitif

Planter's Punch

Makes 8 glasses: Combine $1/2$ cup lemon juice
(about 3 lemons), 2 cups orange juice (about
6 oranges), $1 1/4$ cups pineapple juice, 8 tbs
cane sugar syrup (may substitute 8 tbs cane
sugar) and $1 1/4$ cups brown rum. Place 4 ice
cubes in each glass and pour mix over the top.

Barbecue Party

Hawaiian Style Red Snapper (page 34,
8 servings) or Center Cut Beef Tenderloin
(page 18, 8 servings)

Barbecued Spare Ribs (page 16, 4 servings)

Honey-Crusted Chicken Wings
(page 28, 4 servings)

Grilled Corn on the Cob (page 12, 8 servings)

Grilled Potatoes (page 12, 8 servings)

Aperitif

Coconut Dream

Makes 8 glasses: Blend 3 cups pineapple juice,
2 cups orange juice, 8 oz canned coconut
cream, 8 oz heavy cream and $3/4$ cup lemon
juice (about 4 lemons). Place 3 ice cubes in
each glass or, even better, crushed ice, and
pour mix over the top. If desired, add $1/2$ tsp
Grenadine syrup to each glass. Refrigerate
all ingredients beforehand.

Dessert

Mascarpone Cream

Pour boiling water over 1 pound apricots, remove peels and pits and cut into quarters. Marinate in 2 tbs sugar, 4 tbs lemon juice and 6 tbs orange liqueur. Combine 1 pound Mascarpone, $1/2$ oz whipped-cream stabilizer (available at supermarket or specialty store) 6 tbs powdered sugar, 2 tbs lemon juice and 1 tbs orange liqueur. Distribute apricots and marinade over 18 ladyfingers (5 oz). Spread Mascarpone mixture over the top and refrigerate for 2 hours. Garnish with amaretto.

Dessert

Tropical Fruit Salad

Peel 2 mangoes and cut flesh away from pit. Peel 1 large pineapple, quarter lengthwise and cut out core. Cut pineapple into bite-sized chunks. Marinate fruit in 4 tbs lime juice and 3 tbs cane sugar. Sprinkle with grated coconut.

Or prepare grilled bananas (page 46).

Dessert

Cheesecake

Knead together 6 oz crumbled graham crackers and 2 oz softened butter. Press into a greased pan (10 inch diameter) Refrigerate for 30 minutes. Stir together 14 oz cream cheese, 8 oz sour cream, 5 oz sugar, 3 tbs lemon juice and 3 egg yolks until creamy. Combine 3 tbs cornstarch and $1/2$ tsp baking powder and stir into mixture. Beat 3 egg whites until stiff and fold in. Spread cream onto graham cracker crust and bake for 50 minutes at 350°F.

No-Stress Timetable

1 week before: Buy drinks, Mozzarella and seasonings.

2 days before: Buy meat, vegetables, fruit and prosciutto.

1 day before: Buy fish and bread. Prepare olive caper sauce and dessert. Prepare pork tenderloins.

4 hours before: Prepare vegetable skewers.

1 hour before: Prepare lamb chops and fish fillets. Prepare drinks.

No-Stress Timetable

1 week before: Buy drinks and seasonings.

2 days before: Buy meat, chicken, vegetables and fruit.

1 day before: Buy shrimp fish and bread. Marinate pork steaks.

4 hours before: Prepare papaya sauce, fruit salad, shrimp and fruit-juice rum mix.

1 hour before: Prepare avocado dip and salmon.

No-Stress Timetable

1 week before: Buy drinks and seasonings.

2 days before: Buy vegetables.

1 day before: Buy meat, fish and bread. Cook mango sauce. Prepare spare ribs. Marinate steaks and chicken wings. Bake cake.

4 hours before: Prepare potatoes and corn.

1 hour before: Prepare drinks and red snapper.

The Author

Annette Heisch has always loved cooking and baking. Once she completed her studies in food science, she built her career around food and drink. In 1995, after many years as an editor at famous women's and food magazines, she began working in Munich as a cookbook author and freelance journalist. Her main interests are fast, elegant dishes, healthy and enjoyable fitness foods, regional cuisine and merchandising.

The Photographer

After training as a food photographer and completing several internships, in 1995 Brigitte Sauer began working as an independent photographer for various publishers, magazines and advertising agencies. Most of her work is in the area of food and lifestyle photography.

Photo Credits

FoodPhotographie Eising, Martina Görlach: cover photo
Stockfood: page 4, 1st and 2nd photos from left; page 5, top row, photo on right and 2nd from left; page 7, 1st and 2nd photos
Weber Grills: page 4, 2nd photo from right
petra electric: page 4, photo on right
All others: Brigitte Sauer,

Nuremberg
Published originally under the title Grillen © 2002 Gräfe und Unzer Verlag GmbH, Munich. English translation for the U.S. market © 2002, Silverback Books, Inc.

Editors: Jonathan Silverman, Birgit Rademacker, Stefanie Poziombka

Translator: Christie Tam

Reader: Bettina Bartz

Layout, typography and cover design: Independent Medien Design, Munich

Typesetting and production: Patty Holden, Helmut Giersberg

Printed in China

ISBN 1-930603-02-9

ABBREVIATIONS	
approx	= approximately
oz	= ounce
tsp	= teaspoon
tbs	= tablespoon

Enjoy Other Quick & Easy Books

Coffee and Espresso
Tanja Dusy

Christmas Cookies

1 Pan—50 Muffins

Preserves and Canning

Irresistible Fondue
Angelika Illies

Cooking for Two
Cornelia Adam

Napkins

Fast Italian
Margit Proebst

Sushi
Andreas Fürtmayr
Classic ideas from Japan and new fusion sushi
Home-made perfectly

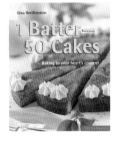
1 Batter—50 Cakes
Gina Greifenstein
Baking to your heart's content

Cooking in Clay
Healthy Recipes with Great Flavor
Erika Casparek-Türkkan

1 Noodle, 50 Sauces
Everyday Pasta • Old and New Italian Dishes
Noodle biography • 10 Tips for Success

Grilling
Antje Gruener

Sauces and Dips

Soups
Classic to Contemporary
Sebastian Dickhaut

Raclette
Claudia Schmidt
New Recipes with Cheese Primer and Party Dips

Antipasti and Tapas
Mediterranean Appetizers
Cornelia Schinharl

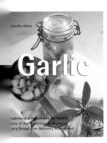
Garlic
Cornelia Adam

Salads
Cornelia Adam

Sandwiches

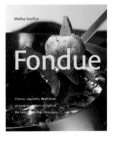
Fondue
Marlisa Szwillus
Cheese, vegetable, & all kinds of meat—cook them all right at the table from these showpieces.

Quiche
Cornelia Adam

SCHEDULING

➤ Light the grill well in advance. It takes at least 30 minutes to develop good coals in a charcoal grill.

➤ Prepare side dishes with longer cooking times (such as potatoes) and place them on the grill far enough ahead of time.

➤ When grilling meat, start with the pieces with shorter cooking times so your guests will be taken care of sooner.

Guaranteed Grilling Fun

HYGIENE

➤ Leave raw foods in the refrigerator until just before you're ready to grill them.

➤ Don't return grilled food to the same plate which held raw food.

➤ A special precaution for poultry: After marinating, throw away the marinade that came in contact with the raw meat. Brush the poultry with marinade that you set aside beforehand.

MARINATING

➤ The marinating time for fish should be brief, usually no more than 30 minutes.

➤ Hearty meats such as steaks, spare ribs and chops can be marinated the day before.

➤ For more tender cuts, such as fillets, don't marinate for more than 4 hours.

➤ Cover marinated food with plastic wrap and refrigerate.

SAFETY

➤ Set up the grill on a stable surface.

➤ Never pour lighter fluid onto coals that are already lit. This could result in unruly flames.

➤ Never use alcohol.

➤ Never leave the grill unattended.

➤ Always keep a bucket of water handy.